WHY $ALES FOR ATHLETES

JOYCE JOHNSON
NICHOLAS WILLIAMS
DARIUS BUTLER

WWW.SELFPUBLISHN30DAYS.COM

Published by Self Publish -N- 30 Days

Copyright 2020 Joyce Johnson

All rights reserved worldwide. No part of this book may be reproduced or transmitted in any form or by any means electronic or mechanical, including photocopying, recording or by any information storage and retrieval system without written permission from Joyce Johnson or Joyce Johnson Enterprises.

Contributing Authors: Nicholas Williams & Darius Buttler

Printed in the United States of America

ISBN: 979-8-63258-751-8

1. Educational 2. Sales 3. Athletes 4. Skills 5. Informative

Joyce Johnson *Why Sales for College Students*

Disclaimer/Warning:
This book is intended for lecture and informative purposes only. This publication is designed to provide competent and reliable information regarding the subject matter covered. The author or publisher are not engaged in rendering legal or professional advice. Laws vary from state to state and if legal, financial, or other expert assistance is needed, the services of a professional should be sought. The author and publisher disclaim any liability that is incurred from the use or application of the contents of this book.

CONTENTS

Acknowledgements v

Introduction 1
Chapter 1: Why Sales for Athletes? 3
Chapter 2: Leadership 9
Chapter 3: Lights Out (Last Game Played) 17
Chapter 4: Accepting It's Over................... 21
Chapter 5: Finish What You Started — Education. 27
Chapter 6: Finding your Zone 37
Chapter 7: From Field to Field — Why Sales?..... 45
Chapter 8: Selling Your Brand 51

Dear Athlete 59
Appendix: Information on U.S. Colleges Offering Sales 63

About the Authors............................. 65

ACKNOWLEDGEMENTS

To my friend, Nicholas Williams (he calls me Big Sis) I love you and appreciate the friendship we have built over the years. Thank you for believing in this project. I only had to ask you once to share your story of love and pain with the sport of football. I don't think either of us knew that writing this book would challenge you to heal old wounds. I hope I captured your big heart in this book and it's a project that makes you proud.

To Darius, it has been a pleasure getting to know you. You are an exceptional athlete and special human being. I believe our first and last call you were in the car picking up your kids from school fully engaged in "daddy mode."

ACKNOWLEDGEMENTS

When Nick called to introduce you to the project, he was so excited that I immediately felt you were our missing link. I am forever grateful for your dedication to this project.

As in every book I want to thank my amazingly, smart, funny, giving and loving family for your undying support and encouragement. My heart is filling up now with joy just thinking of you. I love you so much! Thank you for believing in me and always having my back. To the spouses of this clan—Toni, Tish, Frieda, Britt, Angel, and Margaret, we may not say it enough, but we appreciate and love you. Thanks for putting up with our weird family bond.

In loving memory of my two friends, Joyce Marks and Mia Brown. I am happy we said, I love you and that I was able to be your friend to the end. You are my angels. I miss you and carry your legacy in my spirit every day. Heavenly Hugs.

— **Joyce**

To Joyce Johnson, my "Big Sis" and colleague. Thank you for the opportunity to partner with you and your amazing team to highlight my story, my perspective, and ideas of how we can help the next class of athletes. This book was life transforming for me. Thank you for helping me add to my bucket list of co-authoring a book.

To all the "Supporting Cast" who helped pull this off, thank you. Some of you I have never met, or spoken to, but I know you have been in the background making things happen. I solute you and appreciate all your efforts in making this a reality. This will live on in our legacy!

To my dear friend, Darius Butler, my oldest and longstanding childhood friend. From elementary school to this very point, we've known one another for our entire life-span. I appreciate you coming on board for this feature with Joyce and me. When you told me you were in the next phase of your career, I saw it fitting to extend an offer to join the team. I'm very proud of you as a good father and an accomplished business man. Most importantly, thank you for being "my guy" when I need you. Keep crushing it. The world is ours brother!

I had to save the best for last—my confidant and dear mother, Christine Samuels. You are my biggest supporter, MAMA!!! I love you with all my heart, and want to thank

ACKNOWLEDGEMENTS

you for everything you've done to elevate me, mentally and spiritually. And above all else, thank you for showing me how to hustle. I learned so much about connecting with people, and creating opportunities from watching you when we were growing up. Mom, I love you and hope this book makes you proud.

— **Nick**

First and foremost, I wish to acknowledge my parents, Mitchell and Sabrina Butler, for doing what I believe was a great job of raising me and teaching me the importance of discipline, hard work and helping others. I am also grateful to my kids who make me proud and are often the source for my inspiration.

I am also thankful for all of my friends, family, coaches and teammates who helped me get to the point in life where I am now and who continue to help me grow and go further

Thanks to the readers for buying and taking the time to read this book. It will hopefully provide the beginning tools for success and open their minds to new avenues and possibilities.

Of course, without Joyce Johnson and Nicholas Williams, I might have missed this opportunity to collaborate on such an important project. I am looking forward to doing more in the future.

— **Darius**

INTRODUCTION

Why sales for athletes? Athletes who are able to understand the business of sales will continue achieving high level success earned since those early days of junior high school. As an athlete, you will be confronted with agents, advertisers and friends who will try to "sell" you on why it is a good idea to use your brand to promote everything from t-shirts to mobile phones. You will need to understand the risks and rewards of business ownership, contracts, financials and the best way for you to "sell" your dream idea to partners, investors and buyers. Paraphrasing Billionaire Rapper and Entrepreneur, Shawn Carter (a.k.a., "Jay-Z"), you are not a businessman, you **_are_** a business, Man/Woman!

INTRODUCTION

As competitive as I am, I am not an athlete. As a journalist in high school and college, I interviewed many athletes and covered football, basketball, track, baseball and golf. I worked in the sports information department in college and with the Houston Rockets early in my career. So, I reached out to my good friend Nicholas Williams for his expertise and to ensure we would co-write this book to relate specifically to athletes. Nick immediately expressed a desire to involve Darius Butler. We believe our combined, yet diverse experiences, will provide insight to student athletes globally.

It is our goal that "Why Sales For Athletes" will serve as a guide to inform, educate and engage student-athletes to see the value of converting transferable skills into career opportunities that will prove beneficial in securing well-paying jobs immediately following college graduation, and thereby entering into their best life.

Only two percent (2%) of college athletes move on to play professional sports. Some will realize early on the need for a plan B. Many may not realize initially that an injury has caused their sports career to end, but a good reality check will find them later asking "what's next?" Our goal here is to share options for the next chapter of their lives.

CHAPTER ONE
WHY SALES FOR ATHLETES?

We recommend athletes use their four- and five-year scholarships to study their degree of interest and dual minor in business and sales. If one of these is already your major, take time to get your master's degree. Athletes should always include business studies in their curricula. This is largely because whether it is part of being tantalized by a hugely attractive endorsement deal, considering an alluring enticement to join a partnership, or simply a desire to start a business or non-profit, being armed with basic business knowledge is key to protecting your assets.

SO, WHY SALES?

If only 2% of seven million high school and college athletes will play at the professional level and only 6% will play at the college level, why not take advantage of the 426,261 open professional sales positions reported available in the United States alone? (Indeed.com, January 11, 2020). According to the NCAA, there are 460,000 student athletes in college. Looks like opportunities as sales professionals could help improve if not solve college graduate placement rates. However, that is another conversation. For now, we stay focused on instituting our plan B.

You can say you heard it here, although we may not admit it, but it seems high time for schools, colleges and professional leagues to offer educational training in business and sales to their athletes. This valuable information is beneficial to anyone's future. Good sales training should also include how to properly promote one's personal and/or business brand, as well as pointing out how lucrative a profession in sales can be. The opportunity to become a well-paid professional athlete can be very elusive, but the odds on becoming a renowned, professional salesperson may be closer to realization, as indicated by the statistics.

The goal here is to prevent you from moving back "home" and ending up on the couch because your old room has been converted into a man cave or a sewing room. When you left for college, your parents may have been a

WHY SALES FOR ATHLETES

little teary-eyed, but when they got over it, they looked forward to you coming back for a _visit_—not to move in! It will totally dawn on you when they ask, "With all that expensive education, why are you not employed?"

Sales is about people and building relationships. Friendships, sororities, fraternities, team memberships, roommates, campus clubs and organizations in which you participate can all provide the vehicle toward an inevitable relationship. That means you are already in the business of selling yourself on an everyday basis (i.e., putting forth your best you; promoting your point of view; and perhaps demonstrating the value of what is important to you and why).

What was the last big deal you closed? We are not talking about convincing your parents to buy the latest model Mustang or getting that popular girl to go out with you. This is about what you have done in anticipation for the end of that multi-year college scholarship. How close are you to playing your favorite game? What did you do to prepare for that goal? Have you done all you can to ensure that you are within that coveted two percent (2%) in order to proceed to the professional level?

While we encourage you to google other definitions, we see sales as the art of listening and building any given relationship that gains trust between individuals, while discussing mutual need and fulfillment, allowing one to inform and educate the other about his/her product or service (i.e., solution), and agreeing upon an exchange through a form of payment or results. Simply noted by Oxford Dictionary, "Sales is a transaction of service or goods in return for trade of service, goods or currency."

> RICHARD BRANSON STATED, "IF SOMEONE OFFERS YOU AN AMAZING OPPORTUNITY AND YOU'RE NOT SURE YOU CAN DO IT, SAY YES – THEN LEARN HOW TO DO IT LATER."

Here is some food for thought: this is literally one of the best and biggest concepts in this book. In "The Time is Now" (by Nicholas Williams), the author advises that his brand boasts "Now" because literally the time *is* now. Richard Branson stated, "If someone offers you an amazing opportunity and you're not sure you can do it, say yes—then learn how to do it later." **Now** is prime time to sell your brand with social media and the internet.

Darius is a prime example that even at a small high school in Florida like Coral Springs Charter School, great things can be ahead, if you act ***now***. Small school students, you need not fear; there is actually more competition at larger schools because the evolution of selling yourself at that level becomes that much more challenging.

Note: Among the other great social media vehicles, there is a new platform through which to sell yourself by uploading your brand, promotional recordings, stats and references to "Hudl," a product and service company of Agile Sports Technologies, Inc. This resource provides tools for coaches and athletes to review game footage and improve team play, covering a multitude of sports, including soccer, basketball, volleyball and lacrosse.

The art of the sell, whether self or product, is well demonstrated in a man of whom we are big fans, Shaquille "Shaq" O'Neal, #Superman. He is entertaining, savvy, sincere, smart and one of the best at selling his brand! He has proven that athletes have uniquely inherent skills to accomplish their personal and professional goals. He is a police officer, disc jockey, rapper, actor, sports commentator, entrepreneur, "angel-investor," franchise-owner (Five Guys, Auntie Anne's, a Krispy Kreme franchise, as well as a handful of restaurants, gyms and car washes), CFO (Chief Fun Officer at Carnival Cruise Line), and PhD (yep, that is, **Dr.** Shaquille O'Neal) earned at Barry University. He is also "Top Sales Guy," in my humble opinion; just look at how well he sells anything to which he attaches his name.

During a July 2019 interview with the "Wall Street Journal," he said "The Shaq basketball brand will go away but Dr. Shaquille O'Neal will be forever." For those of us who are his diehard fans, it is doubtful that the Shaq basketball brand will *ever* go away, but we get the picture! However, he has a firm understanding that his sport, basketball, was a tool that provided him access to the people, as well as opportunities, education and lessons in how to position and sell his brand which, in turn, made him an influencer and representative of billion-dollar brands.

Most of us will not have the opportunity to represent or work for billion-dollar companies. However, we can assert the same effort, have access to the same training and become award-winning sales professionals, all according to our efforts. As athletes we have trained hard, for many days, nights and years. We play hard and we play injured and it builds a toughness that is ingrained for life. That toughness will lead you to the top. So, while sales can be tough, you may already possess what it takes to succeed.

It is the goal of this project that by reading to the end of this book, you will be more than ready to write your own definition of sales and how you will use sales to improve the financial success of your brand. You will have a complete grasp of how to sell and just exactly how you will be sold. In this book, you are going to learn the best way to get that job offer, the one that allows you to stay connected to what you have studied, how to earn excellent pay, and how to start working sooner rather than later.

CHAPTER TWO
LEADERSHIP

"Leaders are made, not born."
VINCE LOMBARDI

Coach Lombardi, now there is an influ-encer, and the reason behind the creation of this publication, "Why Sales for Athletes." Many athletes already possess the ability to influence others to make buying decisions. A part of that influence is a given, as a result of your talent, leadership and winning attitude. Those attributes carry weight on and off the fields and courts. Another part of your influence is driven by natural confidence and the passion to support those supreme beliefs. All of the above qualities are infectious

LEADERSHIP

and key to helping you become hugely successful as a sales professional.

In sports you have team captains, quarterbacks, point guards, pitchers, coaches and other staff in leadership roles. Each player on a court, field or otherwise is required to display leadership skills and prepare to make decisions that support the team in case of injuries, change of position or other coaching decisions. The same applies in sales.

Many salespeople are natural leaders carrying a daily dose of enthusiasm and one of those magically motivational notes in their back pockets. Athletes have heard words of wisdom and motivational quotes from the best, their coaches and mentors. The top sales leaders are the best storytellers, and if you were to be listening in the proverbial locker room, field or court, there is a story being told that applies at each phase of the sales process. Let's talk about how to use those teachable moments to sell products, services and *you*!

🏆 **[NICK]** *My experiences in leadership started in high school as the captain of the football team under the guidance of Coach Frank Hepler. Listening to the guidance of Coach Hepler and his leadership had a lot to do with the development of my interpersonal skills.*

Your interpersonal skills include:

- active listening (no one talks when the coach is communicating the game strategy)
- teamwork (be happy for the teammate who scores)
- responsibility (admit when you are wrong)
- dependability (be consistently early for practice)
- leadership (be the example of what to do when coach is not around)
- motivation (point out the brighter side of a losing play

In business, you will often hear terms, such as, "soft" skills, which include:

- flexibility (willing to change plays or positions under coach's direction that have always worked for you in the past)
- patience (gracefully waiting for that chronically late teammate)
- empathy (understanding the coach is under pressure when his blowup seems inappropriate)

LEADERSHIP

All of these, interpersonal and soft skills, are important and needed to engage customers and build relationships, which is vital in sales.

> 🏆 **[NICK]** *Leadership plays a role in every aspect of your life. It is bearing accountability for every role in your life. Clint Session was one of my team members at University of Pittsburgh, and he was known as a vibrant, assertive leader who played the game aggressively. However, Clint was really best known for his faith. After I was injured, I found myself in a dark place not knowing if I would ever play again. As I sat in my room, there was a knock on the door. It was Clint coming from church. He said he wanted to pray with me because he felt something was really wrong. Since then, I have considered him a true friend and a great leader.*
>
> *Another great leader, who led by his calm and quiet example off the field, was Horatio Blades. When he stepped on the field, however, he became a completely different person. He became a fearsome coach who got results. His game was crazy, but yet he was so quiet off the field and always did the right things. Coach Blades was a true example of leadership, to the point of influencing my decision to go to University of Pittsburgh.*
>
> *Everyone has their own attributes and qualities of "leadership." You will definitely pull bits and pieces from a*

variety of people in your life, which meld together to create who we are today. My coaches, Chris Patten, Charlie Partridge and others, were great men in my life. They taught me a lot of life lessons about leadership and how it transcends into our everyday life. It's important to evolve as a leader.

How do we use leadership skills in sales? First, by supporting the team—something athletes have been groomed to do in all aspects. Whatever level of work or sales experience, everyone can use a little extra help with a proposal, pitch or maybe a simple fist bump to say "good job." Take the locker room enthusiasm to the workplace and use it to build relationships and support the team environment.

Secondly, support your coach. In a business setting, away from the field or court, your coach is now the manager. They are responsible for your success and determine whether or not you make that championship sale. If you are one of the fortunate ones, your manager will shout out the same quotes from famous sports legends that inspired you in the past and impart to you the drive to be great. Your manager will schedule training and partner you with a mentor. You will need to give the same respect and attention to your mentor who is also presenting you with opportunities to lead. Raise your hand to support team initiatives, ask for and accept feedback, meet deadlines, and do not get caught at the water cooler unless you are getting water (i.e., do not get caught up in the gossip machine).

Last, but most important, you should lead by example.

> 🏆 **[JOYCE]** *My brother, Ervin, told his daughter, "You don't try out for captain of the football team." It is a position assigned, and only after you have led by example, getting good grades in the classroom, arriving on time to practice, training harder than most, always being prepared and encouraging others.*

As in sports, everyone in sales who shows up does not necessarily make the team, and only a few of those chosen will have formal leadership roles. With that said, the expectation is that you lead by example no matter what your role, and then, you play to win!

Are you ready to lead? It has been said that people leave managers, not companies. In a *Culture Amp*[1] article entitled, "The biggest lie in HR—People leave managers not companies," a conclusion drawn via the study of data from hundreds of the world's fastest growing companies.

---

1 Didier Elzinga, Founder and CEO of the Culture Amp blog. https://www.cultureamp.com/blog/the-biggest-lie-in-hr-people-quit-managers/

Culture Amp's Chief Scientist, Dr. Jason McPherson, concludes that what organizations need to know about keeping good people is that management matters, but leadership matters more.

Are you leadership material? Good leaders are not necessarily those who are in charge. You can begin to lead from the position of an entry-level job just by your mere demeanor. You can exude leadership qualities from the lowest point in the ranks, all by how you conduct the business within your scope of responsibility. A good leader can float to a position of responsibility in a relatively short time by persistently emanating leadership qualities.

What makes a good leader? To make a good leader, you must stay focused on the collective goals of those with whom you work. Help your team to stay focused. Keep them motivated and be willing to help your team players be the best they can be in order to achieve those goals. Establishing your potential to be a great leader is as simple as helping others to reach their goals, and not hesitating to help those who might actually excel in areas that are not your strengths. It is not at all an unattractive quality to take pride in the good fortune and accomplishments of others whom you have helped.

> THE TOP SALES LEADERS ARE THE BEST STORYTELLERS

CHAPTER THREE
LIGHTS OUT (LAST GAME PLAYED)

Have you ever watched Kobe Bryant's short film "Dear Basketball"? This ***Oscar-*** and ***Emmy-winning*** story, directed and animated by Glen Keane, will touch you deeply. Kobe[2] shares his story of how he fell in love with the game of basketball at the age of six-years old. The message could be considered a love letter, a thank you note, and a farewell salute, or perhaps it was a heartfelt apology for leaving the game. Kobe narrated the piece himself, and you can feel his passion for the game with each word as he explains why he felt it was time to leave.

---

2   Please see Dear Athlete near the end of this book.

LIGHTS OUT (LAST GAME PLAYED)

> "I never saw the end of the tunnel. I only saw myself running out of it… My mind can handle the grind. But my body is saying I have to let you go. And that's alright…No matter what I do next, we both know I'll always be that kid with the rolled-up socks, garbage can in the corner, five minutes on the clock, ball in my hands…Love always, Kobe." **(Excerpted from "Dear Basketball")**

Every athlete will be faced with this decision at some point in their career. You will one day play your last game. It may not look like the 60 points that Kobe pulled off in his farewell game against the Jazz, but you will no doubt experience some of the same feelings.

Bilal Issifou is a college student at North Carolina A&T. He was a high school football player with dreams of playing at the college level. He had early plans to study sports medicine and become a kinesiologist. After sending out many promotional recordings and letters to colleges, he found himself thinking the clock had run out. It took him months of internal struggle to admit to his parents that it was over, because to say it out loud would make it real. During an interview on my podcast, "Let's Talk About It #collegelife," Bilal shared the joy of his last game played. The passion in his voice was so strong and you could feel his love and loss of the sport he had played from the age of 12.

"I remember my last game playing for Page High School in Greensboro, North Carolina against Mallard Creek. I remember it was a slightly rainy night. The stands were filled with friends and family or maybe the whole city. If you ever attended a high school football game in a small city, you know that practically the entire community shows up. Thinking back to those final seconds of the game, we scored what we 'thought' was the winning touchdown at the end of the game. Wait for it! It was called back and we lost. Emotions were high, a brawl broke out and we lost the game. It was a feeling of emptiness knowing that it was my last ever high school football game. At the time, I didn't realize it would be the last time I played football as an organized sport. Thinking back, it's still painful."

After some time, Bilal decided it was time to redirect his energy towards his end game. As much as he loved football, he would enter college to prepare for a career in the legal profession. His dream now shifted to becoming an attorney. He then began completing applications to secure scholarships applicable to his future endeavor. Today, Bilal is a sophomore in a strong pursuit to accomplish his goals in the legal field. Thanks to the Accelerated Pathway to Law School Program, he will earn his law degree in 5.5 years! He is preparing for a summer internship at Goldman Sachs in Dallas. He is also the founder of Kingdom of Youth mentoring program. We have no doubt that this young man will more than surpass his dreams of becoming an accomplished attorney.

> ONE THING THEY ALL HAVE IN COMMON IS EVERY ONE OF THEM REMEMBERS THEIR LAST GAME AND HOW IT FELT.

Over the years, we have had the opportunities to meet, work with and befriend athletes at all levels, high school, college, NBA, NFL, MLB and foreign leagues. One thing they all have in common is every one of them remembers their last game and how it felt. They also share the fear of losing the level of recognition, admiration and success of their legendary sports careers. The drive, desire, passion and commitment to be No. 1 in everything they do never leaves their gut! Those are the qualities that every good manager and company are looking for in the people they hire. They are the qualities that helped Bilal to walk away from the game of football that he loved so much and to channel his efforts into successfully navigating his college career; proving there is life after your last game.

CHAPTER FOUR
ACCEPTING IT'S OVER

Unlike Bilal, the young man whose story was shared in the previous chapter, many athletes have a more difficult time making the transfer from *being* everything athlete to be everything plus an athlete.

🏆 **[NICK]** *It took me awhile to start back watching the game. Some guys still can't watch the game today. It's hard leaving something that you've been groomed for your entire life. My last game played is a blur because I was booted off the field during college after being put on academic probation. I took it for granted in high school that I would be recruited by Division 1 colleges, and that I would have the* *opportunity to play my favorite sport at the college level. I failed, however, to stay focused on what was real. There is a reason we are identified as student athletes. I overlooked the student responsibility of the agreement. (More details in the chapter on education.) After walking off that practice field, everything else faded. I felt like I had gone through some type of shock therapy.*

Acceptance that it is time to walk away from a sport that you have given so much to and received so much from is the hardest thing you will ever do. We all know at least one former teammate, athlete or coach who, ten years later can still be found fighting to accept the inevitable (life after the sport). When you literally eat, breathe and sleep your craft your entire life, it is hard to call it quits.

Sad thing is that a majority of us all think we are going to that next level where we will make millions of dollars. Then you get a wake-up call by "life" that catches you off guard. Imagine your first love breaking up with you. The depth of pain is too hard to explain. It took me a while to accept my fate. So many emotions were provoked with this abrupt ending to the dream. The game I knew and loved so much became painful to watch.

When this happens, it is particularly difficult watching the guys with whom you had played so many times before, continuing on in their careers. It was not resentment, just tough to watch. Though you can be happy for "your guys," it is still difficult when that is not how you pictured your future.

For me, the road to the acceptance came with a lot of trials and tribulations. From concussions to being injured by gun fire that took a year away from me, it was all ultimately overwhelming, and I was never quite the same. While accepting it was all tough, I pulled myself together. I applied all I learned over the years from football, went out and got a job, and eventually built a successful business. Football taught me a great deal and gave me a spirit of accomplishment, and so I applied the same principles to the next chapter of my life. I never knew what I wanted to do, except that I would not settle for that nine-to-five cubical job. The one thing I knew was that I wanted to connect with people.

So, here are some take-aways from Nick's experience:

- Not all sales jobs are nine-to-five. Most sales jobs offer very flexible schedules. Some days are 6 a.m. to 6 p.m. There are some nights with late hours preparing proposals, and other days, everything is done by noon.
- The same principles applied on the playing field can help you become successful off the field as a sales professional and entrepreneur.

ACCEPTING IT'S OVER

> If you show up every day, train, work hard and be the best team member possible, you will be successful!

CONTINUED CHANGE

Nothing presents more changes and challenges than sports. Each game is different. Each play and every competitor requires adjustment in preparation. However, a career in sales is a short second to sports. Sales can also be a very challenging work environment. In sports, you are constantly keeping up with the stats and strategies of the teams you play. In sales, it is your job to read and understand each buyer, their business, the market and why they need what you have to offer. Preparation for each sales presentation requires adjustments to the game plan. You must equip yourself with the stats and strategies of your future consumers.

FOOTBALL TAUGHT ME A GREAT DEAL AND GAVE ME A SPIRIT OF ACCOMPLISHMENT, AND SO I APPLIED THE SAME PRINCIPLES TO THE NEXT CHAPTER OF MY LIFE.

Once you begin working your adaptability and skill to change direction, you will find, in the midst of extreme pressure, how instrumental it will be toward helping you maintain focus on the end result,

WHY SALES FOR ATHLETES

winning! Often, when your company decides to change compensation plans, reorganize business strategies, and/or merge or acquire new business units, employees get so distracted on WIIFM (What's in it for me?) that they lose focus on the game. The advantage in sales is the same as in the game: keep selling, close business deals and get paid.

This is why athletes thrive in the sales profession. We may be leaving organized sports, but we can have just as much fun, be as challenged by the competition and experience just as many wins in sales as in professional sports. If you can conquer this level of change in your life, everything else will be a breeze. Notwithstanding other personal or professional challenges, you can bounce back from a crushing blow like a career path change, as Nick shared earlier in this chapter, when he suffered a huge loss in leaving his sport.

🏆 **[NICK]** *It felt like the heartache in losing the love of my life. Your heart gets set on the dream of playing professional sports, but you simply cannot let the loss of the dream keep you from being able to move on with a plan B. Sales is an excellent plan B that does not require self-reinvention. You can start tomorrow with the skills you have learned in sports and begin making the transition from high school, college or professional sports. If you have already*

> *ascertained that you will not play professional sports, then, by all means, consider sales as option A.*

We understand that the transition from sports can be challenging for both male and female competitors. Many athletes at all levels of competition struggle with whether or not leaving the sport is best for their future. The news media and other sources often highlight the struggles of former athletes. Recently, Athletic Academic Advisor Women's Basketball Coach Joi Walker posted on Twitter (01/18/2020) "I have done interviews with over 100 athletes and I hear the same story over and over again. I was on the couch. I was unemployed. I spent 2–4 years scrambling and working odd jobs. I was depressed. I felt like a failure."

Do not spend your energy focusing on any of these inhibiting scenarios. None of them has to be your story. Take what you have learned in sports and get up every day with success on your mind, then show up, follow up and go sell something! Change is tough, but it has its rewards. As an athlete, you have developed the skills ***and*** the talent to be successful in any arena.

CHAPTER FIVE
FINISH WHAT YOU STARTED —
EDUCATION

In your endeavor to become a super-star professional athlete or the most successful sales person in the country, you will never be able to hide the lasting effects that a lack of education reveals. Whether in sports or in sales, your star will shine brighter when you have vigorously pursued a full education!

🏆 **[JOYCE]** *This year, I began teaching business courses at a local college in Houston, Texas. I asked the students to submit copies of their resumes to help me coach them on their "elevator" pitches. An elevator pitch is a 90-second pitch used to sell yourself to a coach, recruiter or*

> *potential customer. One student shared that he was not a good student in high school because he was an athlete and that required most of his focus. One of the major league baseball teams had planned to draft him as a shortstop; but everything changed when he was injured during tryouts. He now spends his days fishing and attending classes. He also works at a local retail store and boasts that he is the top sales guy every month. This student will need guidance in understanding the value of the course that I will be teaching, as well as the importance of prioritizing his education and how it will prove valuable both on and off the field.*

There are not nearly enough appropriate words to stress the importance of education. The significance of a good education becomes increasingly apparent with age, and sometimes through unfortunate experiences like being perceived as a dumb jock.

🏆 **[NICK]** *I can really relate to this topic, recalling the day coach told me I was ineligible to play my senior season. That shit hit me like a ton of bricks. I had no idea what I was going to do.*

It was a Tuesday, a week away from our season opener, we were playing Marshall University. I was halfway through practice, and I noticed the guy who was responsible for keeping us on track with schooling. He oversaw study hall for all the football players. I thought it was strange that he was on the field, and then I noticed him saying something to coach. My coach then walked over to me and broke the news. He said, "Nick, you aren't eligible to play this season."

At first, I thought it was a joke, I was expecting a big camera crew from that show "Punked." I quickly came to the realization that this was no joke, my heart dropped, I was completely lost! It was one of the worst days of my life. I was urged to leave practice early and go see if I could convince my professor to change my grade and raise my GPA.

After I visited my professor about changing my grade, who had said quite vehemently, "absolutely not," I wandered the campus aimlessly thinking to myself, how am I going to tell this to my mom? I then called my brother to console me, and he jumped right down my throat. I never felt so alone in my life! I finally mustered up the courage to call my mom. That call didn't go well either. She was so disappointed. It was then she said to me, "You better get that damn degree."

This was certainly a low point in Nick's life, but it spurred him on to work harder for his education. It was a proud moment when he received his degree. He had not only persevered through a tough season, but he walked away with valuable lessons that he discovred away from the field.

Many professional athletes have gone back to college to finish their degrees. If you are part of that 98% who will not have an opportunity to play at the professional level, completing a well-rounded education should be your top priority. Not every profession or sales job requires a degree, but if you are an athlete on scholarship, why not take full advantage of the opportunity? After all, the financial trade-off with most universities is that if you play, they pay. Equipping yourself with as much education and training as possible will ensure your success.

"But my major is…," you may argue. It makes very little difference. There is a sales opportunity for you regardless of your major. This is why sales is the best option for most anyone, particularly the college athlete. Why? Sales is fun, challenging, competitive, and yet, flexible. These are similar aspects to what draws most of us to an early interest in sports.

You do not always get hired for what you know, but it is often the potential you show for learning, creativity and enthusiasm that puts forth the image of what a good sales person you can be. How well you tell a story that informs, educates and engages your hiring officer will determine your success in obtaining the job. The job you secure may not seem to coincide with your field of study, but just hold on: you might find more in common than you think. You will enjoy the flexible hours in sales; it allows time for continuing your education.

> 🏆 **[DARIUS]** *I decided after graduation, I would take advantage of some of the programs the NFL offered to their players, the Coaching Clinic and the Broadcast Bootcamp, and it has paid off. My initial and long-term goal was to become a coach after my playing days were over.*
>
> *Coaching: now there is a sales job! Have you ever heard anyone give a better sales presentation than a coach? They have this innate ability to turn a short quote into an hour-long story that will make you step up, cry or quit. Remember when the coach came to the house to recruit you and sold your parents on allowing you to leave home and in some cases move across the country? That takes a really good salesperson!*

Communications or media relations students, the world is yours! You ask how do we know? Communications/journalism was Joyce's field of study. Sales opened many doors for her. She worked for the Houston Rockets doing educational sales, telecommunications, energy and distribution.

We, the authors of this book, have all launched our own businesses and invested in various ventures. We have sold in different cities, counties and states. Sales have taken us away from our homes and out of our comfort zones, and yet, we were able to feel at home wherever we have been. We cannot iterate enough that sales is the door to success and preparation is key.

Let's discuss a few other majors. A popular sales job that you may be aware of is pharmaceutical or health care sales. Did you ever think about the educational background of a person in this field?

As a member of the National Sales Network, an organization focused on development of sales professionals and providing opportunities for additional training and networking amongst peers, I took an interest in the fact that this organization has many active pharmaceutical sales representatives. This particular industry is known for having the most professionally aggressive sales teams.

Curious to understand more about the industry, I engaged in conversations with some of these individuals by inquiring how they got started. The first person I talked to attended college and studied biology with plans to go to medical school. When his medical school plans did not pan out, he took a pharmaceutical sales job in a specialized area of medicine.

As indicated several times throughout this book, the sales industry allows you to continue to follow your passion, even when other approaches become unattainable. Another interest may be in prenatal care, where you can explore sales in an area that creates tools or medicine for

WHY SALES FOR ATHLETES

prenatal care and premature birth conditions. Continuing on an interest in healthcare, there are multiple pharmaceuticals that are used to promote the health of HIV/AIDS patients and others used to decrease pain in cancer patients.

Whatever your area of medical or science studies, if your passion is to cure an illness or to build awareness around an illness, there is a sales opportunity out there for you. Sales allows you to continue learning on the ground floor, to launch your personal platform and to inspire others.

If your major is in psychology and sociology, and you have a firm grasp of human behaviors, personalities or cultures, your skills and insights can lead to developing successful, ongoing relationships.

> SALES HAVE TAKEN US AWAY FROM OUR HOMES AND OUT OF OUR COMFORT ZONES, AND YET, WE WERE ABLE TO FEEL AT HOME WHEREVER WE HAVE BEEN.

The first key to uncovering and closing a sales deal is to build a rapport with your customer. Companies spend millions every year training sales teams on the "how-to" of building relationships and having a full grasp of customer engagement. If you are currently studying many of the psychological assessments within your program to prepare you to identify personality traits and how best to respond, this should provide you with the tools to successfully build customer rapport, an essential tool in sales.

Are you an education major? In addition to selling books, educational software and training programs, many companies have an education-focused business strategy. Education is a key vertical market (i.e., narrow market meeting specific needs of a targeted niche) for many companies which you will often find align themselves with your major, whether it is in your primary, secondary or higher education phase.

As a college student, you may think of education as just the usual: going to school; paying tuition; conforming to a variety of instructors; encountering students; being graded. As a future graduate, you may do better to think of it as a huge business opportunity. Education is a business with a very large annual budget. Begin to walk around campus and educate yourself on the many areas of business. Visit the career development department, investor affairs, public relations, marketing. Ask them who manages their social media.

As you explore the campus, get to know the engineers, then introduce them to the maintenance department guys you befriended along the way. (You will understand why later.) There are companies everywhere selling products and services that cover every area of business. Before you leave campus, get to know the various departments and what companies they trust with their business.

Other vertical markets may include: retail (good for you fashion majors); oil and gas; technology; finance; real estate and/or property management; travel, and many others. Government markets may interest political science majors, and within local and state government, there are, among others, various levels of law enforcement for those who are criminal justice or law majors.

Sales is also offered as a field of study at many universities today. You may consider taking a couple of classes as an elective to learn a few basic concepts and gain insight into the ***why*** of the sales process. Taking a few classes may not guarantee success in the field, but it may help to debunk some of the myths related to sales. We would not like to see you graduate and then end up accepting defeat because you have not found that dream job right away. Remember the saying "When life hands you lemons, you make lemonade"? Launching your sales career will be the best lemonade you ever want to taste!

CHAPTER SIX
FINDING YOUR ZONE

Change comes from within. You have to be willing to open up what is deep inside of you for transformation to happen. We listen to many people talk about how they wish they could go back in time to make better decisions in their lives, but the truth is one change will not guarantee the outcome you want. Change comes with acceptance that it is time to move forward. Having come to a realization that your sports career might just be over for good, at the high school, college or professional level, your thoughts should turn to what is next.

Sales is the logical answer. Keep in mind that nearly every aspect of society has sales professionals, whether in business or in social work, whether in Hollywood stardom or in education, you name it. Think of your favorite things. What would you feel most comfortable selling? Figure that out, then, go for it!

There are two types of sellers: a ***hunter*** and a ***farmer***. Which one are you?

THE HUNTER

There is an old fable often seen on motivational posters about the lion, the King of the Jungle. The story goes, "Every morning in Africa, a gazelle wakes up. It knows it must run faster than the fastest lion, or it will be killed. Every morning a lion wakes up, it knows it must outrun the slowest gazelle, or it will starve to death. It doesn't matter whether you are a lion or a gazelle - when the sun comes up, you'd better be running." The ***hunter*** is the lion. He hunts to eat!

The ***hunter's*** role is to identify those businesses that can benefit from the products and/or services available through his/her company. The ***hunter*** must make calls and/or knock on doors ***daily***. Once an opportunity is uncovered, the ***hunter*** must verify the need by getting in to see the right contact (i.e., influencer, main decision-maker) and inform this key person of their need for what the ***hunter*** has to offer in products and/or services. Once the ***hunter*** truly understands what the customer needs, the ***hunter*** creates a presentation to educate the decision-maker on how his product/service meets the needs of their organization. Once the customer agrees, the **hunter** asks for the business and closes the deal. *Then he eats!*

Sales moves at a very fast pace. It requires a relentless work ethic. Get up every day ready to run the race!

THE FARMER

What comes to mind when you hear the word *farmer*? Does it conjure up a vision of chickens, cattle and other livestock, along with rolling hills of ready-to-pick produce, all of which require plenty of daily chores to keep the farm running? Envision the beautiful fields of crops you see when driving down a rural road. If you look far enough into the fields, you will see workers toiling over the land, clearing any debris, watering it and keeping out any animals or bugs looking to feed off of the land, destined to destroy the crops.

That is the role of the *farmer*. Your responsibility is to take over an existing body of business (i.e., customer base) which was previously sold or contracted by the **hunter**. You are responsible for following up with the customer, producing add-on sales and working through any issues, whether previous or current, and all while providing exceptional customer service. You are required to not only retain business with the customer, but also to grow their relationship and revenue with your company. The *farmer* cares for and hunts within the land he or she protects.

WHERE DO I BELONG?

How do you know what the best role is for you? Have you ever taken a personality assessment? If so, you probably took some time to review it. This is good advice for those of you who have not. Enter cautiously, as you want the reading to be accurate. Start with your weaknesses, but you should not linger there too long. The importance of knowing your weaknesses is to gain an understanding of the areas where you need work in order to build partnerships, identify good resources to assist you, and ascertain areas where you are most likely to lead.

Again, address any significant weaknesses, but apply most of your energy toward your strengths and master those. If you are **good** at persuading others to see things your way, if you are a fast learner, if you possess a great personality, if you know when and how to be assertive and, most importantly, if you are fearless when faced with the word "no," then you are ready for any job, especially in sales. Pull from your athletic training and see how those attributes align with these traits.

Do your homework. Study as if you are watching video recordings for your next game. Take time to have conversations with individuals who work in the profession. If you do not know anyone in the sales field, go to a local company and ask to intern or talk to a local representative. Also reach out on social media to ask any of your friends if they know someone willing to introduce you to the world of sales from their aspect. Review your options and decide who you want to be: a *hunter* or a *farmer*. If you choose wrong, no worries, it can be a smooth transition from one to the other.

HOW WILL YOU BE PAID?

There is a myth that all sales jobs are commissions only. This is not true. Let us be perfectly clear, if it is listed as a sales job and does not offer commissions *and* a bonus plan, walk away. Sales people live for incentives (i.e., money, trips, awards and, yes, even gift cards).

There are a variety of compensation plans ultimately you must decide where you feel most comfortable (i.e., follow your intuition) and where you will find your support as someone new to the role. During that all-important hiring interview, it is not only important to discuss pay, but you will also want to ask about the training and mentorship programs. You must not overthink it, just make the best decision within a given timeframe, having considered all of your options.

SALARY + COMMISSIONS

This payment plan is pretty simple. You receive a base salary and commissions based on reaching communicated sales goals. Commission plans and goals may change, some for the better, others not so much. Some commission plans pay out at 100%, others pay by dollars received or multiple targets met.

DRAW + COMMISSIONS

A draw is a minimum payment an employer will pay you as a ramp-up until you build up enough sales to earn commissions or if you are not meeting a monthly sales target. There are two types of draw payment plans, recoverable and non-recoverable. Recoverable means the employer will deduct what they have paid you on draw once you begin earning commissions. Non-recoverable does not require you to pay the funds back. Some companies will pay you a three-month non-recoverable draw to allow you time to close deals. There are companies that offer a minimum payout via draws; some require you to pay them back, others do not. Many insurance and financial consultant businesses are paid on a draw-plus-commission-compensation plan.

COMMISSIONS ONLY

Commissions only is just what it says. You are only paid if you sell something. Some companies may offer a draw, others will not. In this environment, the payout is normally aggressive to entice you to join the company. Startup companies with small budgets may decide to offer a commissions-only plan. Companies may also ask you invest in your sample kit or materials. Most network marketing companies will require an initial investment from you.

Real estate agents, loan officers, title companies and appraisers are more likely to be paid under this commissions-only-compensation plan. There may be some companies out there that offer only salary or draw alone. Thankfully, these are rare. Some financial institutions pay their loan officers a regular salary; however, most private companies pay on a commission-only-compensation plan. When paid under a commissions-only plan, you are normally in a sales role as an independent contractor. This means you are self-employed, an independent entrepreneur. Even if the company offers training or support, you are still considered an independent.

BONUSES/INCENTIVES

Here is where the fun begins. Most people (people who run companies) believe all sales people are money motivated.

The leaders who really get it understand that it is not the money but what we can do with it. This is where bonuses and really great incentives kick in. Companies create bonus plans and incentives for top salespeople.

ADDITIONAL BENEFITS

Additional benefits offered are medical, dental, and vision insurance, along with savings and retirement plans. Some companies form partnerships providing discounts with retail stores, lawyers, auto dealerships, cell phone providers and more. Take time to review the additional benefits your prospective company offers. You can save time and money. As we say, in sales, time is money.

CHAPTER SEVEN
FROM FIELD TO FIELD — WHY SALES?

Making the transition from the playing field to the corporate world is not a piece of cake. Like anything in life, it comes with its fair share of challenges. In sports, you are not usually handed the starting position in the beginning. Sales is no different. It is a tough, emotional roller coaster, battling injury and competing for the No. 1 spot. You will have to pony up, brush the dirt off from your falls and keep moving forward.

People typically buy into you as the product, not as much what you are selling. They probably already have the option of getting whatever you are selling in a million different places. You must embrace the challenges of connecting with new people and observing how positive vibrations can attract their attention. It is important that you work on shining from within. Focus on a happy moment, hold on to it and walk in the door with the confidence that a joyful heart gives you. That is how you shine.

🏆 **[DARIUS]** *The thought of a cubical scared the shit out of me. I was always of the mindset that I was going to be in the league. It took me a couple years to apply the methodology that both fields (sports and sales) were so much alike. It was all a matter of perspective. I always had an inkling that sales was for me. It was time to take what I learned on the field to succeed off the field, but it took adjustment.*

I changed my outlook on the way I viewed corporate America. Same guy, different point of view. I disciplined myself toward mastering my craft. I focused all on learning to develop relationships. I made myself be the first to say hello to people as I walked by, just so they could feel my energy. On the elevator, I would ask, "How's your day going?" and when departing, I would say "Have a great day!" These little changes implemented along the way helped me develop confidence to approach anyone where I could begin to build a relationship.

What I learned through this exercise was that I was not just changing my outlook, but also affecting someone else's day in a positive way. They could have been having the wrong-side-of-the-bed kind of day, and all it took was for someone to say something nice, or even a simple hello to change the trajectory of their whole outlook. This is part of the core fundamentals of sales.

Corporate America was so tough at first, I remember going in to make a sale and feeling like people were looking at me as though I was that dumb jock. I knew I had a lot to prove to the world and most importantly to myself. At one point, a young lady who was a coworker was paired with me all the time simply because she was a bit more articulate than me. I lost confidence during that time because I did not know how to deal with being underestimated.

I was so used to dealing with things from a physical standpoint which was to take frustration out on the football field, but of course you cannot do that in an office setting. I would be jailed, and the story would be all over the evening news. So, what I did was channel my frustrations into my craft, and I focused on learning all the tools that would work toward making me better at it. I started really centering on understanding the market that I was in, so in essence, it would be like spending time in the film room to improve my game on the field.

As a former defensive lineman, I was in the trenches battling men who weighed 300+ pounds. I used to call it "the people moving business;" enough push and pull will leave you on your butt when you go up against someone bigger and stronger than you. That is life, sometimes you just end up on your butt. Time to get up and dust yourself off.

FROM FIELD TO FIELD – WHY SALES?

In sales, it is a numbers game. In order to get better, you keep trying. Study the moves of your opponent, or in this case, what pleases your "prospective client." The goal here, as on the field, is to win. You go to your potential client knowing all you can about their business and its background. With the power of the internet and social media, it is fairly easy to research people, their businesses and what drives them. "Trying" is a heck of a lot more than making phone calls or sending emails. It is important to come up with unique ways and strategies to achieve your ultimate objective.

> **IT IS IMPORTANT TO COME UP WITH UNIQUE WAYS AND STRATEGIES TO ACHIEVE YOUR ULTIMATE OBJECTIVE.**

You must learn to make presentations that are relatable to the prospect, down to the detail, having researched their schooling, sports affiliation and upcoming or past trips they have posted on social media. Darius exemplifies best outcomes through the creative practice of sending recorded videos to clients saying he stopped by their office. They are just short recordings taken in front of a client's physical business location, with charismatic presentation, requesting a meeting. People love creativity!

Persistence also pays off. Think about how many times throughout your day that products are consistently thrown at you through public media. If you see and hear something enough, you will eventually think about giving it a chance.

Day one of practice on the field or in the gym is already a competition, you are being watched and judged for everything you do. "The eye in the sky never lies" is a reference made toward the cameras recording a practice. Sales is the same thing. You are on a team, vying for that No. 1 spot, and competing just to get on the field. It is all about persistence and dedication to your craft. The guys who put in more work after practice and treat every practice as a championship game will be the ones who win the starting roles. In sales, it is all about going the extra mile, doing more, making ten more calls after 5:00 p.m.

Leave it all on the field. Live up to your full potential!

CHAPTER EIGHT
SELLING YOUR BRAND

As we began to write this book, a historical ruling took place. On September 30, 2019, during a telecast of The Shop: Uninterrupted, an HBO show hosted by high school phenom and NBA star, LaBron James, and his business partner, Maverick Carter, it was announced that California Governor Gavin Newsom signed the Fair Pay to Play Act (SB 206) into law, which allows any college athlete to benefit financially from his or her own name, likeness and image. We believe everyone will benefit from this ruling.

Why?

- College athletes will earn money from their brand allowing those needing to send money home to do so.
- College athletes may decide to play longer at the collegiate level.
- It will improve college athletic graduation ratings.
- It allows more opportunity for current professional players to stay longer in the game.

The "Fair Pay to Play Act" is a short step up for athletes transitioning into sales. It provides even more incentive for college athletes to perfect the art of selling their brand, to gain a full grasp of the rules in the business world and to execute forward momentum.

This long overdue act, now that it is here, may require some tweaking, but it is a great option for the sports world. In an area where you are often judged as being only as good as your last game, athletes at any stage of their career should be able to earn additional income by promoting their brand while actively playing.

🏆 **[NICK]** *I can remember one summer when Darius and I had no groceries. Student athletes deserve to have money to cover food, as well as other college expenses and activities. There are many expenses outside* *of tuition, room and board. We were not able to have home-cooked meals, let alone go out to dinner. Date? Well, only if she is paying. Everything was postponed to when we could get that first paying contract.*

Many are defeated by lack of funds. There are college athletes taking out student loans just to be able to buy personal items. Some athletes are also struggling to send money home because they cannot focus in school knowing their family is doing without.

As they endeavor to improve the "Fair Pay to Play Act," the NCAA should also address first contact value (the college scholarship). Has a value already been assigned to us given the amount of our scholarship? What is the actual value of the scholarship? Why can I not leave one college for another or take the money remaining on that scholarship or use a percentage of the funds for living expenses, like coaches are privileged to do.

The pushback response is to get a job to curb expenses, but how realistic can that be after the typical college athlete spends hours in practice, more in additional training and conditioning, time spent in classes and game travel? We are preaching to the choir, as the old adage goes. Let us all take an active approach to secure a better experience for the future of the student athlete.

Let us be part of enlightening college players in the

area of finance like the NFL does for its professional athletes. It is imperative to get the education before the money starts rolling in; especially now that there are so many opportunities to go out and sell your brand to companies, social media or to just start your own business. It is just as important to understand money management as it is to learn the sales process.

BE CREATIVE

By far, Darius wins the "How to sell yourself" creative prize. Have you ever heard of someone creating a basketball dunking video to secure a college football scholarship? That would be Darius Butler, friends and fans! His mother (who was, incidentally, the real MVP) told Darius if they are not calling, it's because you haven't gotten their attention. This guy decided to make a video of himself dunking a basketball, and it worked! Darius realized then that he had to sell himself to get what he wanted. He used the video as his elevator pitch to the world of college football. He introduced himself, built a virtual relationship, highlighted his overall athletic ability, asked for the opportunity to meet and, when the chance came, he closed the deal. This, my friends, is the art of the sale.

> **IF THEY ARE NOT CALLING, IT'S BECAUSE YOU HAVEN'T GOTTEN THEIR ATTENTION.**

> 🏆 **[DARIUS]** *Keep your brand alive and consistent! As I continue to pursue a full-time broadcasting career, my brother and I have created an online show on YouTube entitled "Everything DB." Hosted by <u>D</u>efensive <u>B</u>acks, Darius and Denzel Butler. Pretty clever, eh? Many of you have created and maintained a web or social media presence for years. Now that you are working this thing called adulthood, it might be time to rebrand your social media channels.*
>
> *I started out dunking a basketball to garner attention from top college football programs. Today, I use my expertise to educate followers on the intricacies of playing defensive back. I could have stayed with the standard format. Instead, I decided to risk creating a niche program committed to teaching and encouraging others about the positions I played. Among my followers is Mr. Prime Time himself, Deion Sanders.*

How you decide to sell your brand is up to you. We recommend you take time to think your plan out, do your homework and seek professional guidance. The game off the field is changing. Opportunities, not just to earn money, but also to create job or career prospects for yourself, are expanding. Sales will help you prepare by sharpening your presentation skills, providing insight into the market, helping you to master tips in negotiating the best job, deal or business to help yield the best income.

YOUR BRAND OR THE PUBLIC'S

Everyone needs to concentrate on perfecting a personal brand, starting with high school (maybe even earlier) continuing through college and on to professional life. These days, it is not an easy thing to keep under one's control. It can, at times, be risky, uncomfortable and unfamiliar.

Social media or the **IoT** (Internet of Things) allows "everyone from high-school classmates to existing and future employers, clients and/or old love interests to find information on you and, from those resources, create and publish their own presumed version of who you are. With that said, herein lies the opportunity for someone else to sell a faulty reinvention of you. It is imperative that you create and control the narrative of your brand, lest someone else decides to create your story and sell it as a true biography of your life." Quoted from "Why Sales for College Students," Chapter Three, "How to Sell Yourself: Reinvention," by Joyce Johnson.

Personal branding is a process and approach by which you create your own narrative using your skillset, expertise, proficiencies, actions and achievements to obtain the desired result, thereby positioning you for that ideal university, professional athletic position or top sales job. A personal brand, on the other hand, is a common perception, and oftentimes **mis**conception, of who you are based on information known to the public. Your personal brand is too frequently the expression of what others say about you, and can prove to be out of your control, if not carefully guarded. When it comes to having the future you most desire in sports and in sales, you must remain vigilant about your public persona.

DEAR ATHLETE

Dear Athlete,

I hope this note finds you having fun! Thank you for reading "Why Sales for Athletes." My goal is to help you prepare for life after sports. As we finalize copy on this book, historical, life-changing events are taking place around the world. I want you know that, hey, things happen. How we respond is what lands us on top. As a sales professional, I have the toughest, most rewarding job there is, and my success is highly due to my ability to adapt to change. During my time in the oil and gas industry, it has collapsed maybe three times (versus every 20 years as once forecasted), the real estate market has crashed, and at the time of this writing, much of the world's business is at a standstill due to the COVID 19 outbreak. Yet, my ability to stay focused and adjust my game plan to keep selling continues to land me on top of my game.

Many of you will be impacted as the world's leaders seek to find a solution to cure or at least put up a good fight against the current pandemic. Schools, professional sports leagues and major events like March Madness have all been paused or canceled. Some of you were looking forward to the opportunity to seal an NBA invite as a result of participating in the games that are now canceled. Our local Houston high schools are missing opportunities to play at the state championship level, as games will be rescheduled or canceled for this year (2020). Athletes from smaller schools were hoping for an opportunity to play in front of college and NBA recruiters.

We have a saying in sales—"Close Early"! You don't want to wait until the end of the month, quarter or playoffs to hit your goal. Now that unforeseen challenges are taking place, review your plan, check it well and adjust accordingly. Stay focused and don't give up.

You have listened to coaches give speeches since you were ten years old or younger on how preparation + confidence = winning! As athletes, if you put in the time and preparation needed to be the best in your sport, you will win in all areas of life. If there was ever an athlete that led by example showing the discipline it takes to be the best on and off the court, it was Kobe Bryant. After we finished the first draft of this book, we lost NBA legend, mentor, mentee, husband, father, and son, Kobe Bryant (August 23, 1978 – January 26, 2020), #BlackMamba. NBA owners, past and current players and fans from around the world are grieving the loss of Kobe Bryant, his daughter Gianna and seven others killed in a horrific helicopter crash in Southern California.

Kobe's Mamba persona is often talked about in speeches of perseverance and leadership from youth camps to corporate boardrooms. It's been said that Kobe's work ethic and ability to redirect his thoughts to vision-positive outcomes were his strongest attributes. As you embark on your journey after high school, college or professional sports, you may experience a range of emotions from excitement to fear. During those times think of #BlackMamba mindset and go to work.

"Great things come from hard work and perseverance. No excuses."
— Kobe Bryant

Thank you for reading "Why Sales for Athletes." I wish you the best on your journey to success. Before getting started, define what success is for you. I recommend you make it less about money and focus more on your talent, resources and others you can help along the way. Let me know how it goes or if I can help. Connect on LinkedIn at linkedin.com/in/joycej or other social platforms @iamjoycejohnson.

Make it a great Life! Start today!

APPENDIX
INFORMATION ON U.S. COLLEGES OFFERING SALES

Featured snippet from the web: Best Sales and Marketing Colleges in the U.S. for 2020:

Rank	School Name	Ranking
4	Northwestern University	Based on 40 review
5	Georgetown University	Based on 32 reviews
6	Vanderbilt University	Based on 28 reviews
7	Harvard University	Based on 44 reviews

Sales Education Foundation's Knowledge Center:
https://salesfoundation.org/knowledge-center/

INFORMATION ON U.S. COLLEGES OFFERING SALES

Sales Education Foundation's Sales Education Annual 2019 https://salesfoundation.org/wp-content/uploads/2019/04/SEF1901_2019Annual_FinalforWeb_Digital_LoRes.pdf

Study.com: Best Schools for Aspiring Sales Professionals 2020 https://study.com/articles/Best_Schools_for_Aspiring_Sales_Professionals_List_of_Top_US_Sales_Schools.html

Courses in Sales in USA 2020 https://www.academiccourses.com/Courses/Sales/USA/

Colleges with Sales and Marketing https://www.google.com/search?q=COLLEGES+WITHSALES+AND+MARKETING&rlz=1C1SQJL_enUS863US863&oq=COLLEGES+WITH+SALES+AND+MARKETING&aqs=chrome..69i57.15015j1j4&sourceid=chrome&ie=UTF-8&ibp=htl;splinter&sa=X&ved=2ahUKEwiirfextcznAhVmhXIEHUf8CWsQiYsCKAF6BAgUEBI#htivrt=splinter&htidocid=LyhxQ8YmOc7k43d8AAAAAA%3D%3D&fpstate=tldetail

ABOUT THE AUTHOR

JOYCE JOHNSON

Author, Speaker, Sales Influencer and Business Coach, Joyce Johnson has over 20 years of experience as a "Corporatepreneur." She started her sales career in professional sports and later entered the telecommunications industry leading to a role as Sales Director in global markets and worked to deregulate both the telecommunications and energy markets. Joyce spent the past six years in the distribution industry as a National Account Manager earning top recognition as the #1 seller in 2017 and 2018. She recently left corporate and founded "Why Sales Network" to market her brands as an author, professional speaker, trainer and business coach.

ABOUT THE AUTHOR

Over the years, Joyce has managed double duty as a corporate sales leader and entrepreneur starting her first business to support professional athletes in marketing their brands. She would later become a full-time business owner and COO for the National Basketball Retired Players Association's Miami Chapter and supported other brands including; Harris County Flood Control District, Space Center Houston and many others.

Passionate about mentorship and student development, Joyce has published several books: *Why Sales for College Students*; *Top 10 Sales Tips for College Grads*; *Get A Job Today — 5 Things You Need to Know*. She hosts a podcast "Let's Talk About It #collegelife." Recently, she submitted an entry to "Vivianite — A Collection of Inspirational Stories," entitled "How to Sell Your: Reinvention." She is a board member for LIT College Tour and hosts other college events most recently the Bahamas HoopFest (Women's NCAA Division 1 Tournament) and is planning a 2021 Spring Track Invitational for the Bahamas.

For additional information visit www.iamjoycejohnson.com, or follow Joyce on LinkedIn at www.linkedin.com/in/joycej.

NICHOLAS WILLIAMS

Nicholas Williams is a serial entrepreneur, with millions in revenue generation to date. A former collegiate athlete, Nick began his career in sports marketing, where he worked with top-tier athletes to create off-the-field opportunities with a philanthropic edge. After several years spent building brands for sports figures, Nick shifted gears to the tech industry. He developed relationships and worked with some of the largest brands in the world, including but not limited to Nike, GNC, Merrill Lynch, Ameriprise, Tesla, Moët Hennessy, ESPN, Gatorade, Metro PCS, Miami Dolphins, Miami Heat, MDLIVE, Coastal Wealth, Met Life, Where Magazine, Verizon, Captivate, Zimmerman Advertising, Max Borges Agency, just to name a few.

As CEO-Founder at NOW Interactives, Nick strategically aligns clients with the best solutions for collecting data and creating additional revenue streams. NOW Interactives boasts a vast network of Fortune 500 companies, with whom they have facilitated deal flow while serving as a business development arm for emergent companies. "We're dot connectors, who help businesses grow and introduce large companies to innovative solutions that may not be on their radar," says Nick. He is also the co-founder of (FOI) Faces of Innovation; which is a newly founded group of industry leaders. FOI creates

ABOUT THE AUTHOR

uber-luxury networking, and team building experiences through business influencers and technology.

Nick recently launched a tech-investment lifestyle series, The Connectors, which highlights the growth, innovation, and culture of the tech ecosystem. The Connectors will be produced at the No. 1 technology PR agency in the US, Max Borges Agency. The show will feature informative and engaging conversations with business leaders and founders in their respected industries.

Nick also devotes whatever free time he has to volunteering and coaching at Niklaus Children's Hospital, Voices for Children, Cypress Creek Football team and Overtown Youth Center.

DARIUS BUTLER

Former NFL Player
Real Estate & Impact Investor
Public Speaker
Philanthropist

Born to Mitchell and Sabrina Butler on March 18, 1986, on a U.S. military base in Frankfurt, Germany.

Darius Butler played cornerback and safety over his 9-year NFL career for the New England Patriots (2009–2010) Carolina Panthers (2011) and the Indianapolis Colts (2012–2017). Butler grew up in Fort Lauderdale, Florida

WHY SALES FOR ATHLETES

and attended Coral Springs Charter School. He continued his education at the University of Connecticut where he was a two-time captain and started all four years as a cornerback. He was an instrumental piece in transforming their football team into a nationally ranked program. Head Coach, Randy Edsall called him "the best athlete to ever play for the program." He graduated in 2008 with a bachelor's degree in sociology and was drafted in 2009 by the New England Patriots.

Butler was most known for his impeccable football IQ and timely playmaking ability. In 124 games played, Butler intercepted 15 passes, made 333 tackles, forced eight fumbles and scored four times on defense during his career.

In 2009, Butler and his family founded The Darius Butler Foundation, a 501(c)(3) non-profit organization, in an effort to give back to the community. The foundation was created to **tackle** hunger in underserved communities, **inspire** at-risk youth to achieve their dreams and **score** in the classroom!

In 2017, Butler was nominated by the Indianapolis Colts for one of the most prestigious NFL honors a player can receive for leadership and philanthropic efforts, the Walter Payton Man of the Year award. The award granted him and The Darius Butler Foundation $50,000 to donate to his community efforts. Through this honor, The Darius Butler Foundation has donated to local food pantries, college scholarships, the Jack Brewer Foundation for computer labs in Haiti, a local little league football team

ABOUT THE AUTHOR

for new state of the art training equipment and stylish uniforms, and to public schools in Broward County for educational and technology programs.

Butler has made guest sportscaster and football analyst appearances on Fox Sports, ESPN, and the NFL Network as he pursues a career in sports broadcasting. Fueled by his passion for educating, inspiring, and motivating others, Butler shares knowledge and expertise learned from his own journey in hopes of impacting and helping those next in line. One way he does this is through public speaking initiatives that allow him to touch the lives of others and present his authentic self. In partnering with the platform Let's Engage LLC, Butler has had the opportunity to not only realize this passion, but to also fulfill it with hopes of expanding his reach to more audiences.

In retirement, Butler has begun to explore real estate opportunities. As founder and CEO of Butler Estates LLC and TDH Development LLC, his investments thus far have been exclusively in single-family homes with plans to expand to commercial projects by 2020. Butler currently serves on the board of directors for Memory Trees, a 501(c)(3) community and economic development corporation that provides technical, educational and financial social investment services to improve the conditions in lower-income communities. Butler is currently enrolled at the Gabelli School of Business at Fordham University pursuing his Executive MBA degree.

www.ingramcontent.com/pod-product-compliance
Lightning Source LLC
Chambersburg PA
CBHW050251220526
45465CB00002B/643